The
Cup
of
Goodness
by

Rich Beechler

Illustrated by
June Sand

junesandart.com

Dedication

This story is dedicated to the child I never had the opportunity to share it with.

Acknowledgments

With great appreciation to

John Millunzi

Who encouraged me in the path of writing, and seeing something in me that I didn't see.

Robert Ward

Who read my work and encouraged me anyway.

Margy Gish

For battling over every word and sentence until we finally accomplished the task: converting this mountain into a mole hill.

June Sand - *junesandart.com*

Whose artistic skills brought reality to a fictional story, opening a new world into the minds of children.

Joy Houseman

For her additional editing skills.

And

William Moore "Foothill Bill"

For Layout

A path borders the thorny branches once heavy laden with berries, now covered with a diamond blanket of newly fallen snow reflecting the moon's early morning light. To the right, flows the slowly meandering Minnow Creek. Continuing left to Knobby Hill, down to the right, is Old Man Willow, weeping with sickles of ice reflecting the start of the new day.

This pathway leads to the meadow of Piney Forest where we find the burrow of Jack the Rabbit.

Jack lay in his mother's arms, looking through the burrow window at the first fallen snow. Icicles hung glistening in the window as he saw the sun begin to shine. Today wasn't just an ordinary day, it was his birthday, and none of his friends were there. That was because Jack had moved to a new burrow, and all of his friends were back in the old neighborhood that he had known so well. Even though today was Jack's birthday, he didn't have anyone to play with, and he was sad.

As he lay looking through the fur of his mother's arms, he was thinking what a lonely day it was going to be without his friends, and wondering how his day was going to be any fun. Just then, through the window, he saw his father pulling up in his Bunnymobile. As the doors opened, his friends began pouring out of the car! Jack happily realized that he wasn't going to play alone today.

He ran to the door, laughing with glee as they greeted him with shouts of joy and presented him with gaily wrapped presents.

Mother Rabbit took the packages and stacked them all together on the table, and then she turned to the kitchen to begin baking cookies and a birthday cake.

All the kids squealed with delight as they watched Jack open his gifts.

First there was a kazoo, and everyone took a turn. Then they bounced the ball and picked up the jacks. They spun the top, and began playing all the games like Pin the Tail on the Bunny, Carrot Pickup Sticks, and Bunny Office.

Suddenly it dawned on Jack the Rabbit that someone was missing. He wondered where was Bunny Bunny? He didn't ask anyone where she was, but he was concerned because of all his friends, Bunny Bunny was the most special. She would not have missed this day unless something was wrong.

He walked quietly over to the window, and as he stood staring out, his frown of concern turned into a huge smile when he saw Bunny Bunny hop out of her father's Bunnymobile. As she hopped through the burrow entrance, giving Jack a wide smile, he told her he had been worried because he knew she wouldn't have missed his birthday. Handing him his present, she assured him that everything was all right. She explained that she was late because she had to finish washing the dishes and cleaning her room before she could come to the party.

Sitting down with all the kids, Jack opened Bunny Bunny's present and was surprised to see exactly what he had always wanted – a pair of sunglasses that were just like hers! Everyone went back to the games that they had all been enjoying so much. There was laughter and joy, giggling, screaming and fun.

Looking up, he saw Bunny Bunny waving him over to the window where she was standing. She was staring intently at something under the tree across the yard.   Not seeing clearly what it was, he suggested they go outside. They went quietly so as not to disturb anyone as they made their way out the back burrow entrance. It was a blue jay, half buried in the snow, tired and shivering from the cold. Jack picked it up and warmed the bird in his paws. He asked the bird its name, and why it hadn't flown south for the winter with the other birds months ago.

The bird told Jack that his name was Bob the Bluejay. After a few moments in the warmth of Jack's furry paws, he remarked that Jack and Bunny Bunny seemed kind, gentle and full of goodness, and he wondered if they would mind doing him a favor. Curious, they looked at each other and agreed to help. Bob explained, "Mean and Nasty are on the way to Mother Natures' house to spill the Cup of Goodness. Mean and Nasty are dark feelings that hide in shadows and are invisible. They jump into hearts and minds and make us feel mean and nasty. Then we don't want to do good or kind things. Just for the fun of it, they like to go around making trouble whenever they can, such as playing tricks and getting others into trouble.

Any time in the world that someone wants to do kind things, goodness is spilled out to them from the Cup of Goodness by Mother Nature. We need to find her and warn her because they are on their way."

With this mission in mind, Jack the Rabbit, Bunny Bunny Rabbit and Bob the Bluejay began searching for the path to Mother Nature's house. They looked behind the burrow, past the tree line and Old Man Willow, and there, fallen across Minnow Creek, was a hollow log.

Jack cautiously entered the log, with Bunny Bunny and Bob following quietly behind. Emerging from the log, the three little ones stared in awe as they saw before them a wonderland.

This magical place was bright with sunshine and dotted with gaily colorful flowers scattered between mossy green hills. Trails wound their way lazily through the beckoning knolls. Jack commented that they surely must be close to Mother Nature, as this was a most beautiful place, and Bunny Bunny quickly agreed.

Bob asked Jack and Bunny Bunny if he should fly ahead to do some scouting, and see if he could find someone to guide them on their journey. He assured them that he would return immediately when he learned something. Jack and Bunny Bunny agreed and told him to be careful.

Bob flew ahead in search of help and soon he encountered an alligator by a pond. Cautiously he approached the alligator, who was sunning his belly in the warmth of the morning sun, "Excuse me, sir. My name is Bob. Jack, Bunny Bunny and I are looking for Mother Nature's house. Can you help?" Slowly the alligator rolled over and displayed a big smile. "My name is Ally, and it will be my pleasure to give you directions." Happily, Bob flew back to get his friends.

Meanwhile, Mean and Nasty, had found a way to hitchhike by hiding inside Jack and Bunny Bunny. When Bob arrived he told his friends that he had found Ally the Alligator, and Ally would give them directions.

Hearing this, Mean and Nasty jumped from their hiding places and rushed ahead and entered the alligator. The three friends merrily made their way to Ally, unaware of what had just happened. When they arrived, Jack asked Ally, "Can you tell us the way to Mother Nature's house?"

To their surprise, he growled viciously and snorted that he might just eat all three of them then and there.

Frightened out of their wits, they ran
for a path to safety.   Mean and Nasty
immediately returned to hide inside Jack
and Bunny Bunny.

Ally quickly realized what had happened, and couldn't believe what he had done. Ronny the Raccoon, who had been watching the whole thing, asked Ally, "Why did you do that?" Ally admitted that he had no idea and didn't understand what had gotten in to him. He said, "I have never been so mean and nasty." He asked his friend, Ronnie to run ahead and beg Jack, Bunny Bunny and Bob to forgive him, and Ronnie set off at once.

When Ronnie reached the trio, he relayed Ally's message and begged their forgiveness, assuring them that Ally had never behaved in this manner before. They quickly forgave Ally, and eager to get on their way again, they asked Ronnie if he would like to join them in their journey to find Mother Nature. Ronnie enthusiastically agreed.

As before, Bob Bluejay flew ahead of the others in search of someone to help them. While they were walking the winding trails, Jack and Bunny Bunny explained to Ronnie that one of Mother Nature's gifts was sharing goodness throughout the world. When someone wanted to do a kind deed, goodness was sent out to them. Every time goodness is used, it comes back and refills the ever flowing Cup of Goodness. Jack and Bunny Bunny told Ronnie that it was urgent that they find Mother Nature because Mean and Nasty were on their way to her house to spill the cup and do away with Goodness in the world forever.

Meanwhile, flying ahead looking for someone to help give directions, Bob Bluejay came upon a troll who introduced himself as Terry. After a pleasant exchange of greetings, Bob asked Terry if he could give them directions to find Mother Nature's house. Terry said yes, and Bob set off to bring his friends. Returning to Jack and Bunny Bunny, Bob shouted that he had found Terry the Troll ahead, and he would give them directions. Hearing this, Mean and Nasty again left their hiding places in Jack and Bunny Bunny and swooped into Terry Troll.

When the travelers arrived, Jack said, "Hi, Terry, we are the ones looking for Mother Nature's house. Can you give us directions?" Terry, for no reason known to himself, shouted at them, "Who do you think you are? I should eat you all in one bite right now."

Frightened again, they madly dashed off, narrowly escaping to another trail. Mean and Nasty swooped out again and hid inside Jack and Bunny Bunny.

Back at the knoll of Terry the troll, Lenny Lizard was waiting for an answer as to why his friend, Terry, had acted in such a terrible way to the guests in their land. Scratching his head in dismay, Terry admitted that he had no idea what had gotten in to him, and why he was so mean and nasty. Feeling ashamed, he begged his friend Lenny to run ahead and apologize for his bad behavior.

Lenny set off at once, quickly overtaking the group, and delivered the request for forgiveness from the troll. Being of a gentle and forgiving nature, they accepted the apology and invited Lenny to join them, and he agreed. Resuming their journey, Jack and Bunny Bunny explained the purpose of their mission in trying to find Mother Nature's house before it was too late.

As morning turned into afternoon, the growing procession finally reached a clearing that opened into a spectacular and even more breathtaking land of beauty. In the midst of this meadow, in front of her house, a radiant Mother Nature stood next to the sparkling Cup of Goodness that dazzled their eyes. The excited travelers beamed with delight at having found her at last.

Crossing the clearing and approaching Mother Nature, Jack began to explain their mission. No sooner had he started to warn her than Mean and Nasty jumped from their hiding place in Jack and Bunny Bunny, and swooped to the rim of the Cup of Goodness. Together they began rocking back and forth, faster and faster, harder and harder as everyone stood in stunned silence.

The Goodness began spilling over the edge, splashing from Mean and Nasty on to the ground as it sparkled and shimmered its goodness. The group of friends that had worked so hard to prevent this watched in horror. Their hearts went empty. They were confused and sad having failed in their quest to help Mother Nature.

Mother Nature spoke gently to them in a comforting voice. "Don't despair. We have accomplished my mission. It had been so long since my children of the world have wanted to do good, that the Cup of Goodness became too full, and I didn't have the strength to tip it myself. So I tricked Mean and Nasty in to coming here to tip it for me. They have now been touched by the goodness in the cup and will no longer be a bad influence in the world.

Everyone was filled with wonder and joy, laughing and giggling with the sense of happiness in the air. After the celebration had quieted, Jack and Bunny Bunny realized that they had been away from home for a long time, and their parents would be worried. Jack said to Mother Nature, "We are in big trouble because we have been gone for so long from my birthday party."

Mother Nature smiled and said to them, "Because you have helped me so much and been so brave, I will send you back in time to the place in your yard, under the tree, in the snow where you first found Bob the Bluejay. As a special gift for your efforts, I will bless you with the memory of this adventure."

With a wave of her hand and a wink of her eye, Jack and Bunny Bunny found themselves back at the base of the tree.

Holding hands, they slipped quietly back in to the party where no one had even missed them.

Made in the USA
San Bernardino, CA
29 February 2020